I0419273

Hobe Sound

Bridge Road Town Center

Project Vision and History

Community Development Department

Martin County Administrative Center
2401 S.E. Monterey Road
Stuart, Florida 34996
(772) 288-5497

COUNTY OF MARTIN · STATE OF FLORIDA

MARTIN COUNTY
Community Redevelopment Agency

Dynamic   Innovative   Sustainable

GOLDEN GATE · HOBE SOUND · INDIANTOWN · JENSEN BEACH · PALM CITY · PORT SALERNO · RIO

MARTIN COUNTY
Community Redevelopment Agency

MARTIN COUNTY BOARD OF COUNTY COMMISSIONERS

District 1	Doug Smith
District 2	Ed Fielding, Chair
District 3	Ann Scott, Vice Chair
District 4	Sarah Heard
District 5	John Haddox

MARTIN COUNTY COMMUNITY REDEVELOPMENT AGENCY

District 1	Doug Smith
District 2	Ed Fielding, Chair
District 3	Ann Scott, Vice Chair
District 4	Sarah Heard
District 5	John Haddox

COMMUNITY DEVELOPMENT STAFF

Kev Freeman, Director
Edward Erfurt, Urban Designer
Nancy Johnson, Community Development Specialist
Pinal Gandhi-Savdas, Community Development Specialist

Dynamic   Innovative   Sustainable

GOLDEN GATE • HOBE SOUND • INDIANTOWN • JENSEN BEACH • PALM CITY • PORT SALERNO • RIO

BOOKS
FURNITURE

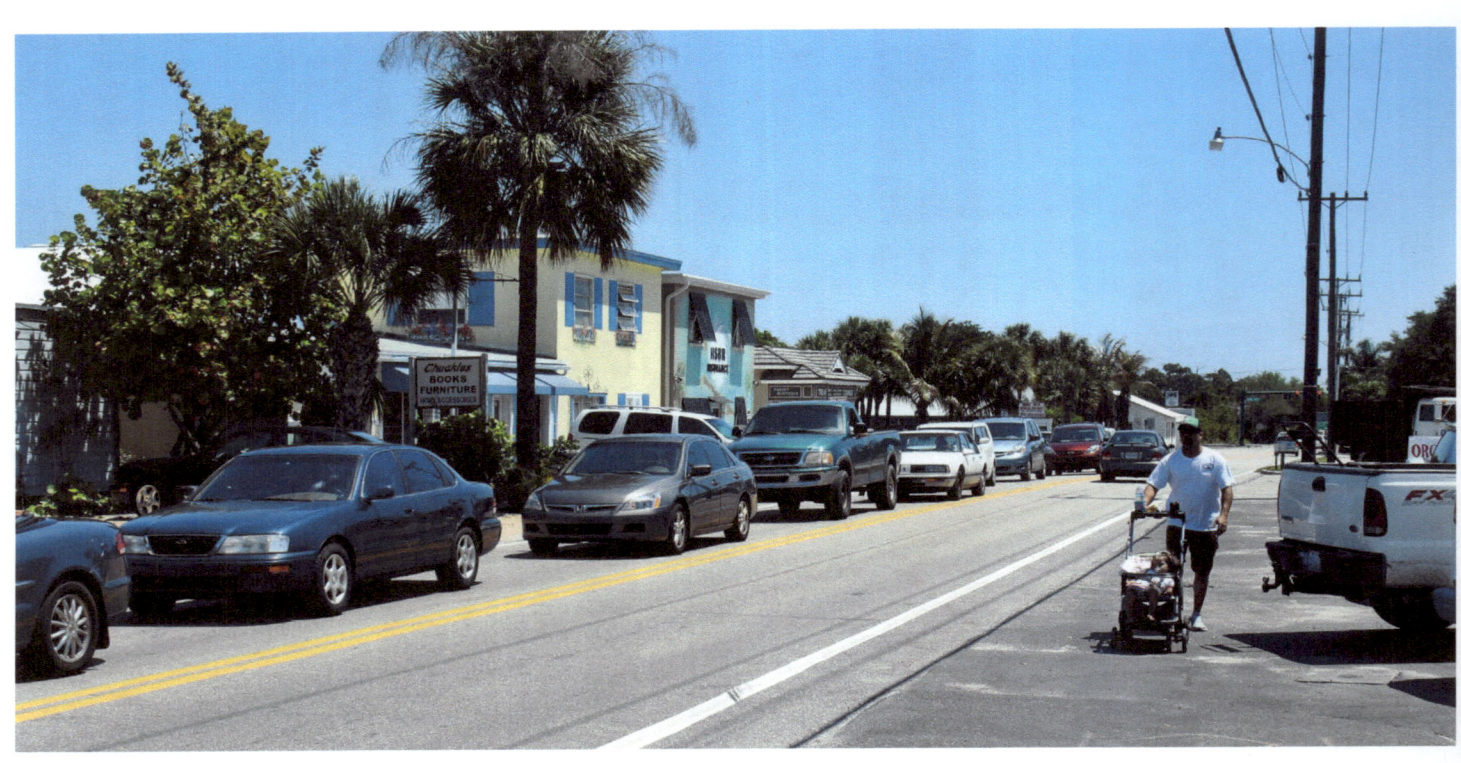

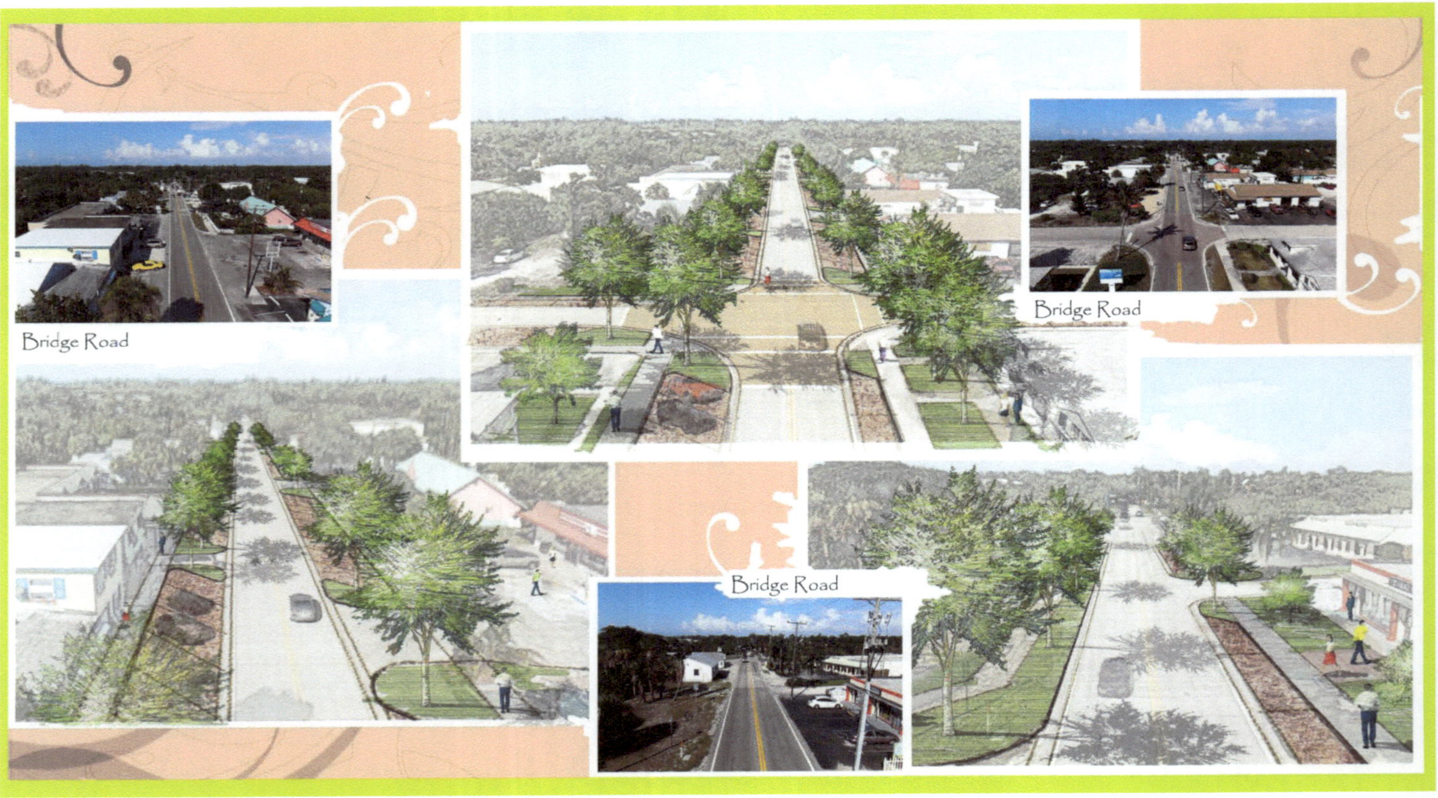
Bridge Road
Bridge Road
Bridge Road

Table of Contents

 **Area Summary**

MARTIN COUNTY
Community Redevelopment Agency

CRA Area: Hobe Sound
Plan Adoption: December 2000
Total Area: 1,024 Acres
Area Highlights:
- Southern Gateway into Martin County from Jupiter Island and Palm Beach
- Access to FEC Rail

Special Designations:
- Mixed-Use Overlay

Hobe Sound

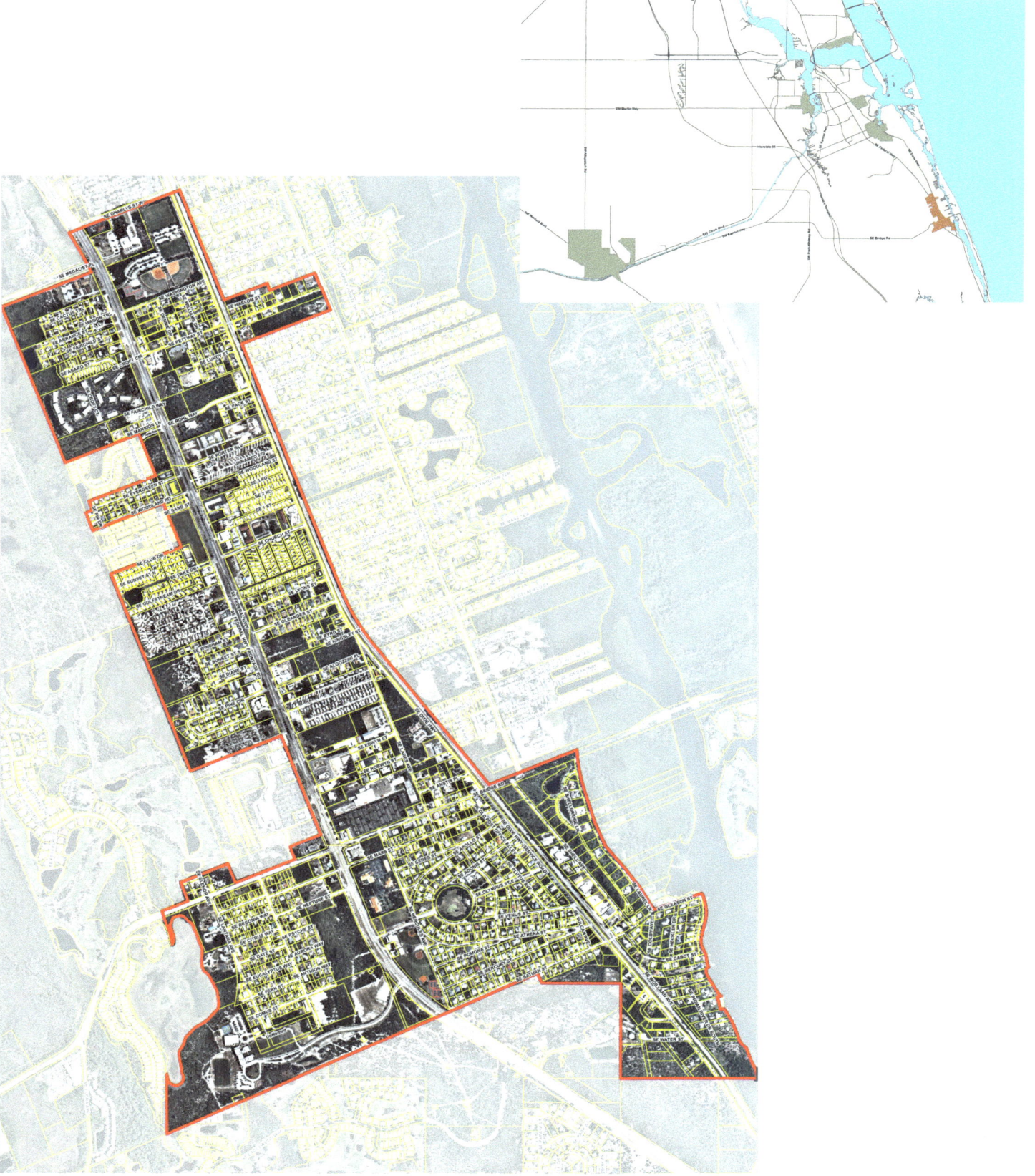

Bridge Road

Bridge Road

Bridge Road

Executive Summary

Bridge Road Main Street

Plans to enhance Bridge Road have been ongoing through the Hobe Sound Neighborhood Advisory Committee (NAC) and the Hobe Sound Community Redevelopment Plan since 1998, with precursor goals identified as early as 1994. Bridge Road was targeted as the #1 focus area in the 2010 NOW Visioning community report. The vision for Bridge Road is that of a sustainable neighborhood "Main Street" setting that will support a vibrant downtown for all.

On November 18, 2010 the Hobe Sound Neighborhood Advisory Committee (NAC) directed Community Development Department (CDD) staff to look at improvements to the Bridge Road corridor. Study objectives included:
- Evaluate parking configuration to increase the amount of parking stalls available
- Improve vehicular and pedestrian safety
- Evaluate the undergrounding of overhead lines and consolidation of utilities
- Add sidewalks for walkability
- Reduce speeds
- Address unique conditions and needs of existing businesses

Following this directive, staff held a public workshop on February 10, 2011 with property owners and business owners along the Bridge Road Corridor as part of the initial discovery phase. From this meeting staff developed two to three conceptual drawings for each property in conjunction with the individual property owner or business owner. These sketches were prioritized over the next several months and formed the basis of the conceptual plan for the corridor.

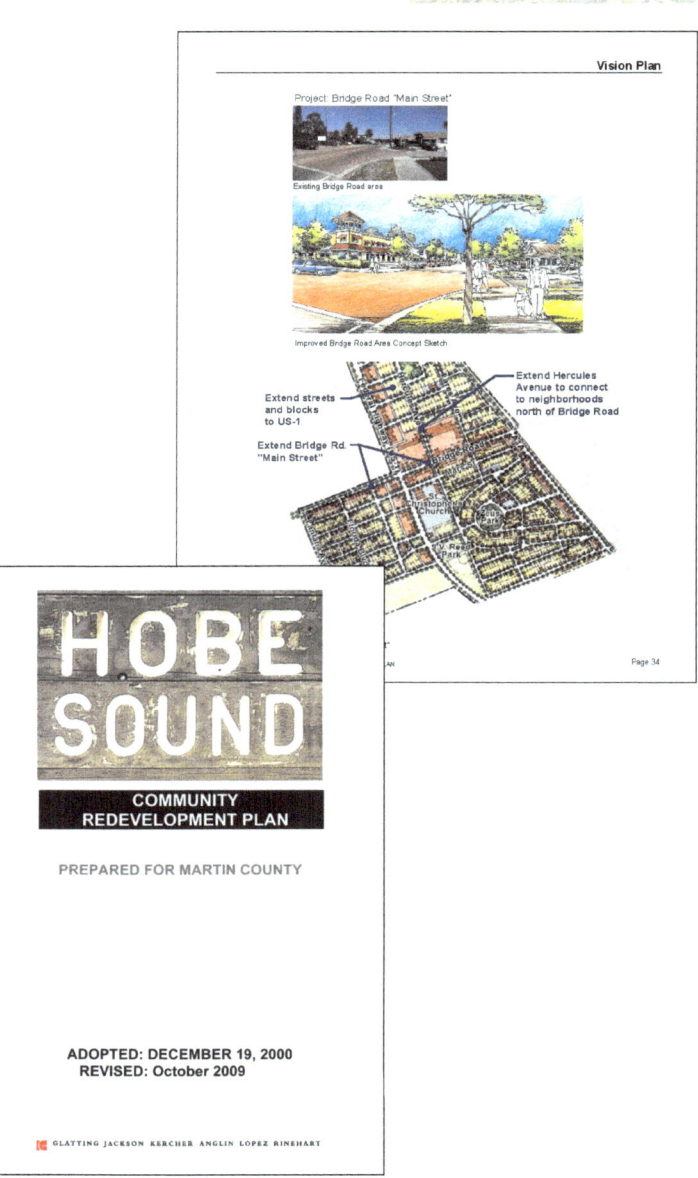

The conceptual plan was proposed and unanimously accepted by the Hobe Sound Neighborhood Advisory Committee at their September 22, 2011 meeting. Community Development staff was next instructed to pursue a contract for 100% construction drawings that would include parking facilities, underground electrical distribution, underground franchise communication, relocation and consolidation of potable water main, stormwater management facilities, roadway improvements, and aesthetic improvements along the corridor.

Perspective Location '1' Existing Corridor

Perspective Location '1' Improved Corridor

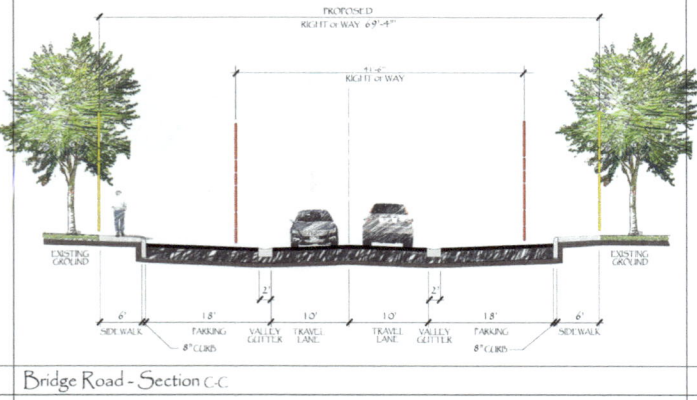

Bridge Road - Section C-C

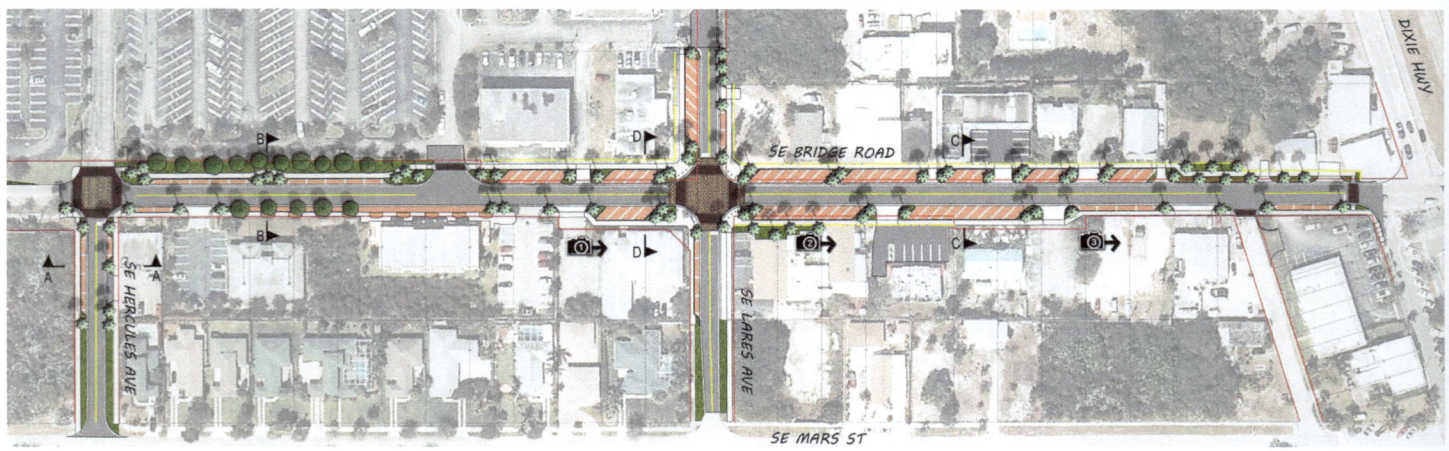

Environmental analysis, geotechnical report, title search and right of way abandonment were completed as of March 2012 in cooperation with Martin County Engineering Survey and Property Management Division. The acquisition of necessary right of way to ensure alignment of the corridor and implementation of project elements as outlined in the conceptual design plan. The Hobe Sound NAC motioned for staff to proceed with the initiation of Right of Way donations necessary to implement the project at their September 22, 2011 meeting. The Martin County Board of County Commissioners approved the acceptance of all future Right-of-Way donations at their May 08, 2012 meeting. Construction drawings went underway in 2013.

In March 2014, staff met with property owners and business owners along the Bridge Road Corridor to gather site specific feedback on how the project will impact their business/property. The staff provided detailed design including parking, signage and streetscape enhancements for each property along with the corridor design plan. For most part, the property owners understood the benefits of the project and wanted the CRA to proceed with the plan.
The following concerns were identified during the meeting with individual property owners/business:

- Losing existing designated parking spaces available on lot and how it will impact tenant getting occupational license
- Signage alternatives
- Head out parking vs. head in parking
- Density impact with land donation
- Donation agreement are lengthy and complex
- Prefer construction to begin in summer vs. during season

The staff continued to work with property owners in addressing their site specific concerns. The comments that staff received from the property/business owners were provided to the consultant (Brian Good, Kimley Horn) to see how we can modify the design to accommodate the changes requested.

FPL requested easement within the parcel located in the Bridge Road/Lares Avenue to provide for the necessary transformer box to be located within the parcel. This would remove sight line impediments from the Bridge Road/Lares Ave intersection and help consolidate easements into one parcel. We scheduled a multiple calls with FP&L, property owner (who lives out of state) and staff to identify location for the transformer box within a private parcel. The owner agreed to provide easements on private property. This was a huge success in order to achieve hardening of utilities.
In March 2014, staff met with South Martin Regional Utilities (SMRU) to discuss the proposed Bridge Road Improvement Project and the opportunity to replace the water service lines that are outdated. SMRU agreed to run some models and cost estimate to replace the potable water main lines and identify budget for the project.

The County received 90% drawing plans in July 2014. Due to limited TIF funds available, the project will be completed in phases. The next step is for the consultant to provide construction plans for Phase I, which will include undergrounding of utilities, improvements on Service Road and improvements at the intersection of Bridge Road and Dixie Highway. Additional phases are to be completed as additional TIF funds becomes available in the future. Since the project cancelled, all work has stopped.

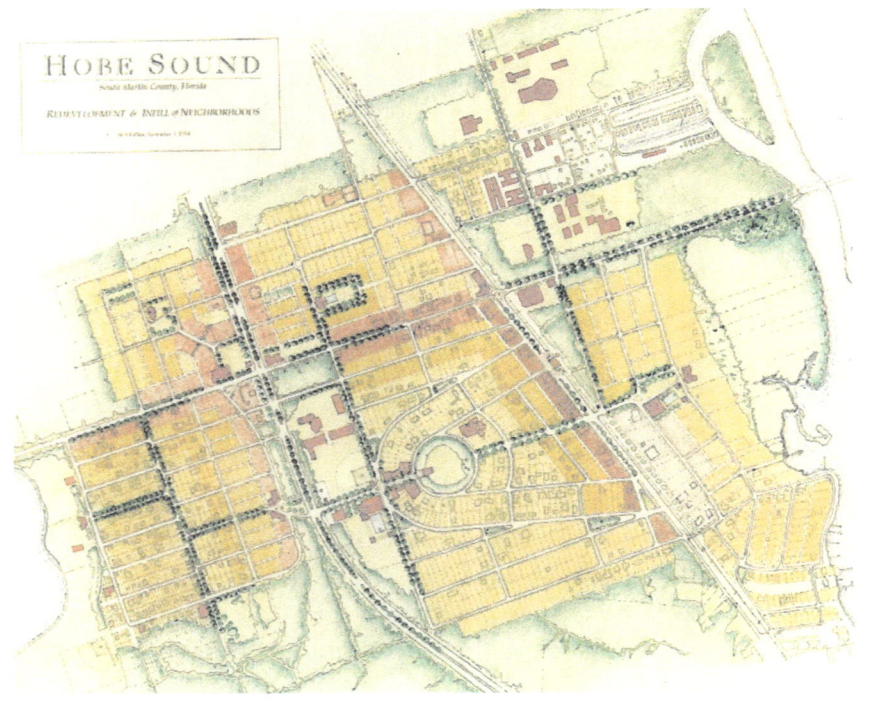

HOBE SOUND
South Martin County, Florida

REDEVELOPMENT & INFILL of NEIGHBORHOODS

SOUTH MARTIN COUNTY

CHARRETTE REPORT

Prepared by
TREASURE COAST REGIONAL PLANNING COUNCIL

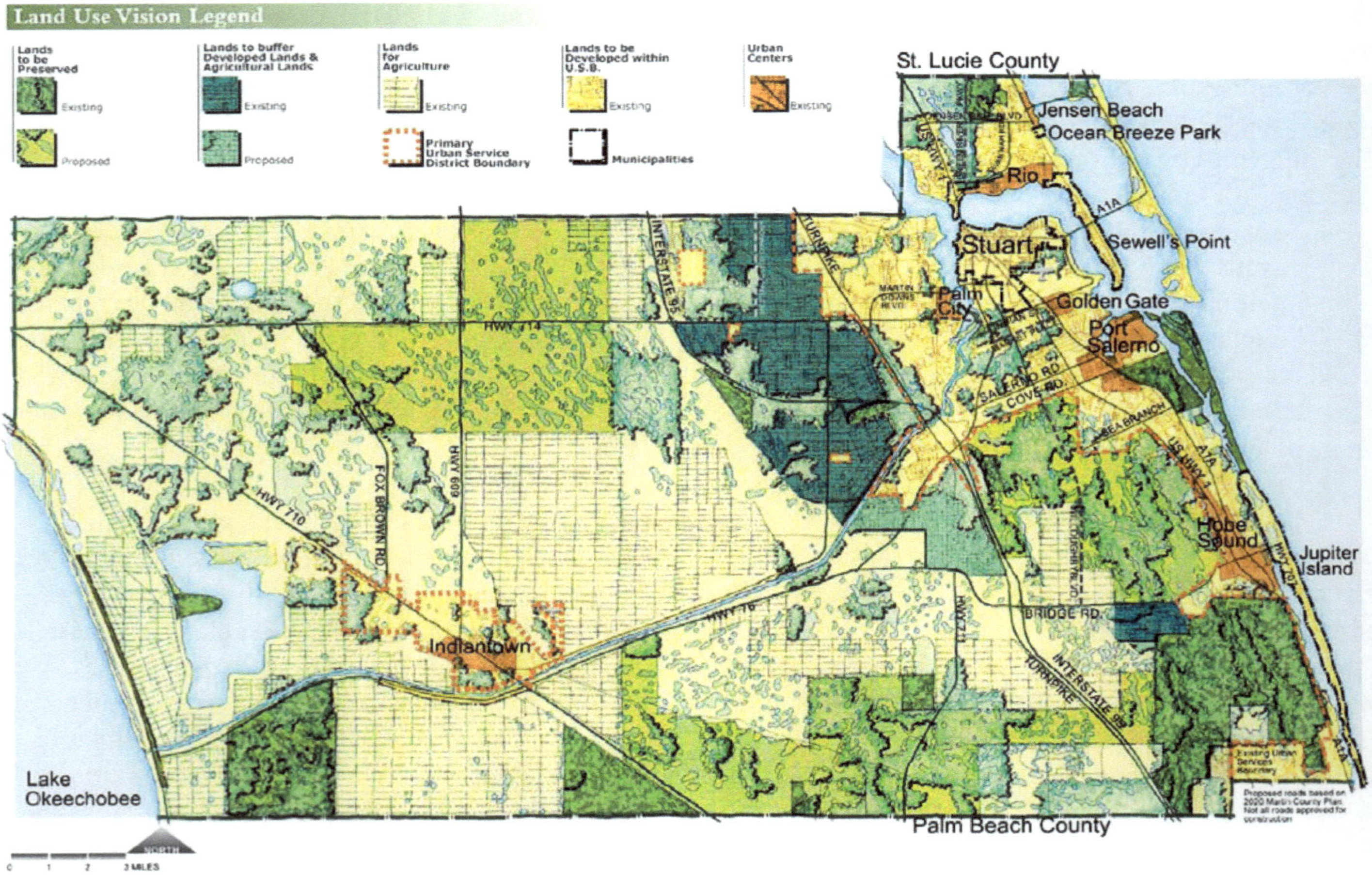

Land Use Vision Legend

Lands to be Preserved
Existing
Proposed

Lands to buffer Developed Lands & Agricultural Lands
Existing
Proposed

Lands for Agriculture
Existing
Primary Urban Service District Boundary

Lands to be Developed within U.S.B.
Existing

Urban Centers
Existing
Municipalities

St. Lucie County

Jensen Beach
Ocean Breeze Park
Rio
Stuart
Sewell's Point
Palm City
Golden Gate
Port Salerno

HWY 714

INTERSTATE 95

HWY 710

FOX BROWN RD

HWY 609

Indiantown

HWY 76

BRIDGE RD

Hobe Sound
Jupiter Island

Lake Okeechobee

Palm Beach County

Proposed roads based on 2020 Martin County Plan. Not all roads approved for construction.

0 1 2 3 MILES
NORTH

8

Project History

South Martin County Visioning Charrette

In 1994, Martin County held the South Martin County Visioning Charrette. The Charrette established a vision for the future development of the southern portion of Martin County. In 1995 the report was adopted by the Board of County Commissions. The plan includes a recommendation to encourage redevelopment of Bridge Road as a traditional Main Street. This recommendation from the Charrette Report formed the foundation for the Hobe Sound Community Redevelopment Plan.

These early plans provided the County and Residents a vision for the future and a focus area for Hobe. Following the adoption of this plan, community members continued to meet to discuss how to advance this community vision. In the late 1990's other neighborhoods in Martin County were explore the Florida Community Redevelopment Act, and the use of a Community Redevelopment Agency to assist in the implementation of this vision.

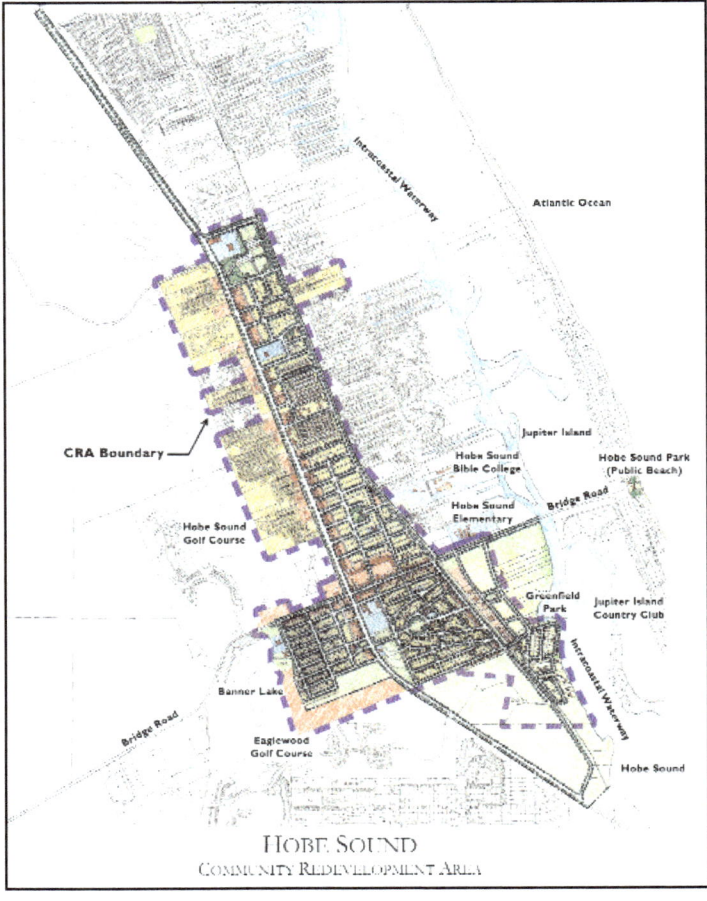

Bridge Road "Main Street"

Cost:
$385,000[5]

Funding Sources:
Bonding/repayment
Special assessment
General Fund

Timeframe:
5 - 10 years

Hobe Sound's public and commercial spaces along Bridge Road and A1A are extremely important assets that define the village character and offer community-gathering spaces. Improving connections between these activity centers and abutting residential areas will greatly enhance the vitality of the area. However, there are a series of additional actions that can be taken to strengthen and further develop this commercial area as Hobe Sound's "Main Street".

Traditional town centers include a mix of retail, service and residential uses within in an area that can be easily traversed on foot. Typically two walls of buildings line the "Main Street". To achieve this comfortable, compact town center in Hobe Sound, the density of uses needs to be increased through in-fill development.

Bridge Road connects US-1 and A1A and forms the "Main Street" of Hobe Sound. While at first glance this corridor contains many of the positive characteristics desired in and along a Main Street, future development along the roadway may work against this image. This is likely to occur if, for example, development along the roadway is permitted to take the form of strip malls set back from the roadway and fronted by expansive parking lots. Properly designed streetscape improvements, including street trees, sidewalks and a modified layout for the existing on-street parking could significantly enhance the pedestrian environment of this commercial area.

The existing streetscape west of Lares Avenue should be extended westward towards Banner Lake Park and eastward to A1A. Extending the streetscape will beautify the corridor and clearly define the sidewalk for pedestrians.

Currently, pedestrians stand on an undefined or non-existent sidewalk between parked cars and Bridge Road traffic. The

cross Bridge Road at mid-block. Angled parking in front of the storefronts will maintain access while allowing customers to back onto Bridge Road in a safer manner. This parking layout re-arrangement will also permit sidewalks to be installed at the front building line.[6]

In the future, as traffic warrants, signalizing the intersection at Lares Avenue would allow pedestrians and traffic to cross Bridge Road in a safe manner.

It is also recommended that Bridge Road remain a two-lane roadway. A roadway with a larger cross-section will only result in separating the uses and pedestrians of downtown.

The community can immediately begin to focus attention on the Bridge Road commercial area as a public gathering space. This could be accomplished by planning special outdoor public events and holiday celebrations to highlight the community businesses and reinforce the district as the Main Street.

Implementation
The Bridge Road Main Street redevelopment can be achieved through a combination of public and private investment over time. Martin County can boost investor confidence by proceeding with the construction of the planned Bridge Road streetscape improvements. The County should also establish design guidelines for the area, and should consider a[n] incentive to façade improve[ments] should be encouraged to up[date] conditions of existing prope[rty] demands through infill busi[ness]

Left: The following images are the supportive planning sheets and referenced diagrams developed by the Hobe Sound Community, recommended by the Neighborhood Advisory Committee, and adopted by the Board of County Commissioners.

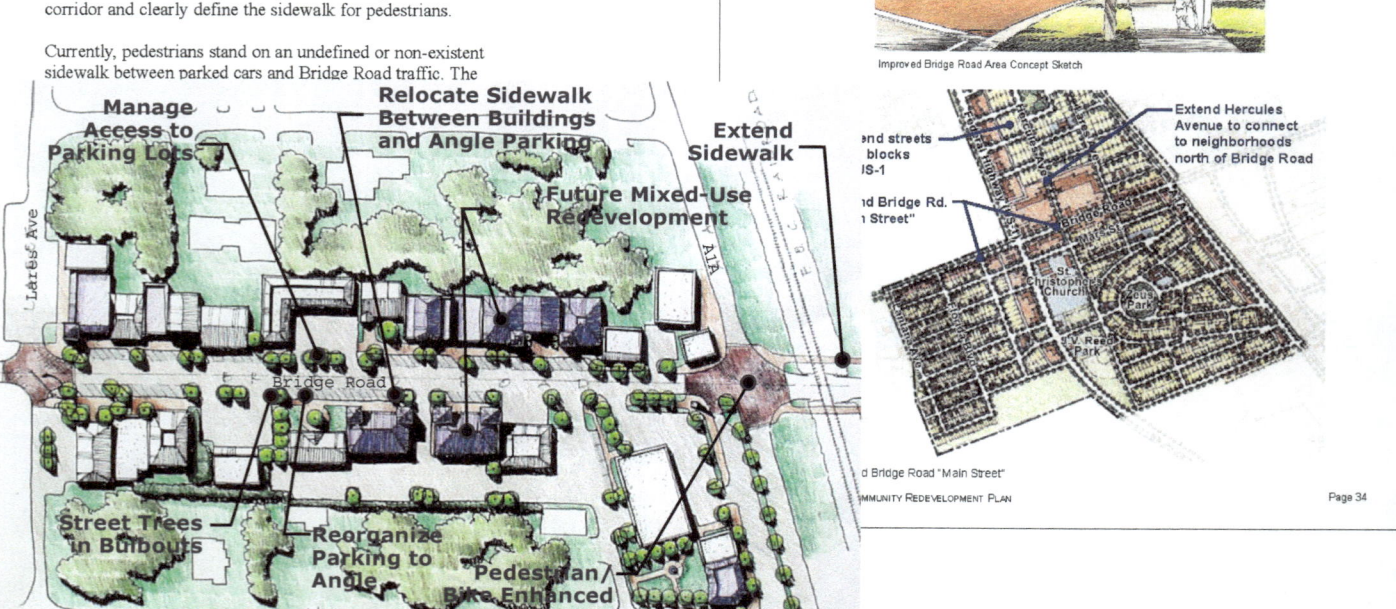

Community Redevelopment Plan

The planning and community workshops for the Hobe Sound Community Redevelopment Area occurred through 2000. The Hobe Sound Community Redevelopment Plan was adopted by the Board of County Commissioners in December 2000.

The Redevelopment Plan was developed with the community in public meetings through the Neighborhood Advisory Committee. These recommendations were organized and prioritized in the Community Redevelopment Plan. The plan intended to be developed over time, as funding became available.

The Hobe Sound Redevelopment Plan identified the Bridge Road "Main Street" as one of the main objectives of the plan. The plan identifies Bridge Road as the center of the commercial main street of the redevelopment area. The plan includes goals that overlap with the Bridge Road project such as the need for neighborhood infill, a focus on commercial development in Town Center, and enhancement to the community connections.

Project: Bridge Road "Main Street"

Existing Bridge Road Area

Improved Bridge Road Area Concept Sketch

Hobe Sound Visioning Charrette 2000:

Saturday, January 22, 2000 Workshop

Seawind Elementary School

Zoning Overlays

The Board of County Commissioners adopted the Hobe Sound Zoning Overlay in September 2001 which supported the community vision through the Martin County Land Development Regulations. These regulations provided the opportunity for small scale infill and mixed-use development in Hobe Sound. The following year, the Board adopted the Hobe Sound Design Regulations which expanded the detail of the zoning requirements to include architectural requirements, and requirements for enhancements in the public right of way. However, the lack of infrastructure made it difficult for the redevelopment of properties on Bridge Road and Dixie Highway.

DGE ROAD LOOKING WEST: CHANGE OVER TIME

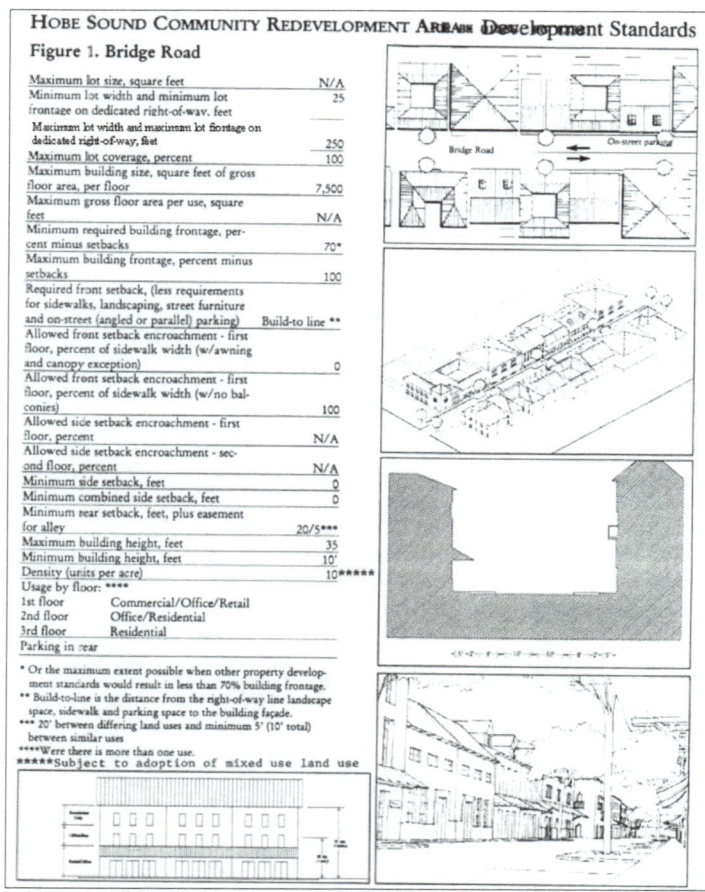

HOBE SOUND COMMUNITY REDEVELOPMENT AREA Development Standards
Figure 1. Bridge Road

Maximum lot size, square feet	N/A
Minimum lot width and minimum lot frontage on dedicated right-of-way, feet	25
Maximum lot width and maximum lot frontage on dedicated right-of-way, feet	250
Maximum lot coverage, percent	100
Maximum building size, square feet of gross floor area, per floor	7,500
Maximum gross floor area per use, square feet	N/A
Minimum required building frontage, percent minus setbacks	70*
Maximum building frontage, percent minus setbacks	100
Required front setback, (less requirements for sidewalks, landscaping, street furniture and on-street (angled or parallel) parking)	Build-to line **
Allowed front setback encroachment - first floor, percent of sidewalk width (w/ awning and canopy exception)	0
Allowed front setback encroachment - first floor, percent of sidewalk width (w/no balconies)	100
Allowed side setback encroachment - first floor, percent	N/A
Allowed side setback encroachment - second floor, percent	N/A
Minimum side setback, feet	0
Minimum combined side setback, feet	0
Minimum rear setback, feet, plus easement for alley	20/5***
Maximum building height, feet	35
Minimum building height, feet	10'
Density (units per acre)	10*****

Usage by floor: ****
1st floor   Commercial/Office/Retail
2nd floor   Office/Residential
3rd floor   Residential
Parking in rear

* Or the maximum extent possible when other property development standards would result in less than 70% building frontage.
** Build-to-line is the distance from the right-of-way line landscape space, sidewalk and parking space to the building façade.
*** 20' between differing land uses and minimum 5' (10' total) between similar uses
****Were there is more than one use.
*****Subject to adoption of mixed use land use

Above The Zoning Overlay supports the implementation of the Bridge Road Improvements through redevelopment.
Right Top The Design Regulations include a series of illustrations and additional requirements to implement the community vision for Bridge Road.

Community Visioning

As the Sewer Project began to come to completion in early 2007, Staff began working with the community to explore how to develop plans for a more attractive "Main Street" in the traditional Hobe Sound downtown on Bridge Road and A1A. The goal of this planning was to provide improvements to the street's look and function so that shoppers are drawn to it and want to spend time moving from shop to shop, as adopted in the vision in the Hobe Sound Redevelopment Plan.

The local resident and Chair of the Neighborhood Advisory Committee, Tom Fucigna, developed a citizen plan that included a comprehensive list of desired features for the downtown Hobe Sound. This work was presented to the Neighborhood Advisory Committee which supported these ideas.

This planning identified specific goals that could be achieved within the existing ROW limits and/ or within an ideal expanded, consistent ROW, and continue pursuing attainment of those goals at every opportunity. The goal is to attain the vision of a sustainable, integrated town and neighborhood setting.

PARKING AND
TRANSPORTATION
IN COMMUNITY
REDEVELOPMENT
AREAS

A case study of the Hobe Sound
and Old Palm City CRAs

September, 2006

Existing parking	
Bridge Road	278
Dixie frontage road	135
Dixie Highway	55
FEC ROW	30
Neighborhood streets	18
Total	516

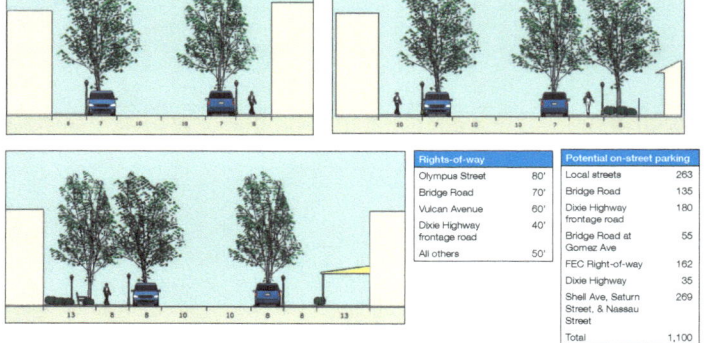

Rights-of-way	
Olympus Street	80'
Bridge Road	70'
Vulcan Avenue	60'
Dixie Highway frontage road	40'
All others	50'

Potential on-street parking	
Local streets	263
Bridge Road	135
Dixie Highway frontage road	180
Bridge Road at Gomez Ave	55
FEC Right-of-way	162
Dixie Highway	35
Shell Ave, Saturn Street, & Nassau Street	269
Total	1,100

Above Exerts from the parking study specific to the Community Redevelopment Overlays for Hobe Sound, including the inventory of existing parking and possible parking configurations.

Parking Study

In 2006, Community Development Department Staff evaluated the parking needs for the redevlopment areas following the principles promoted by famed University of California Professor, Donald Shoup. Shoup's work book "The High Cost of Free Parking," had recently been published which explains how better parking policies can improve cities, the economy, and the environment.

This report outlined a series of key elements needed to implement transportation improvements that are part of the Palm City and Hobe Sound Redevelopment Plans. Such improvements include:

- Generous sidewalks
- Shade trees, benches, and awnings to make the sidewalk more inviting
- Less on-site parking and less of it visible from the main street
- More on-street parking, shared parking among several businesses, parking lots and parking garages
- Encourage more people to walk or bicycle to the downtown area
- Encourage people to park once and walk to multiple stores or offices
- Encourage more compact development and discourage the unnecessary use of increasingly valuable land for surface parking.

The parking study also highlighted the need to create a unified parking code with shared and reduced parking rates for redevelopment, the establishment of a parking trust fund, and utilizing public rights of way for on-street parking to meet redevelopment parking requirements.

This report was shared with the Neighborhood Advisory Committees, local businesses, and local chamber of commerce. These ideas were also implemented into the Martin County Land Code, and utilized in the redevelopment of parcels in the Community Redevelopment Areas.

NOW Visioning

In 2009, the Community Development Department hired a new Director, Kev Freeman. He began a series called the Neighborhood Opportunities Workshop (NOW) Visioning. These two day public workshops provided the residents, property owners, and business owners of the community redevelopment area a venue to share the strengths, weaknesses and opportunities of their community. This public input built consensus on the Recommended Activity Focus areas.

In the case of Hobe Sound the Recommended Activity Focus area was the Bridge Road/A1A Corridor and the Banner Lake Neighborhood.

Specific to Bridge Road, the community expressed the need for the following:
- Master Design
- Small Town Character
- On Street Parking
- Underground Utilities

The NOW Visioning demonstrated that the Hobe Sound community had tremendous pride in their community and that any Activity Focus would need to reflect this pride. Bridge Road is the center of this community and affords the potential of consolidating the 'small town feel' that the community is determined to retain and emphasize. The first Activity Focus should therefore be aimed at cementing Bridge Road as the 'Main Street' of the Hobe Sound community. CRA actions should therefore be aimed at a consensus design approach to revitalize and support businesses.

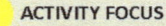 ACTIVITY FOCUS

Martin County CRA

Recommended Activity Focus

1. BRIDGE ROAD/A1A
Master Design
Small Town Character
On Street Parking
Underground Utilities
2. BANNER LAKE
Sidewalks
Infrastructure
Beautification

Recommendation:

The NOW Visioning demonstrated that the Hobe Sound community had tremendous pride in their community and that any Activity Focus would need to reflect this pride. Bridge Road is the center of this community and affords the potential of consolidating the 'small town feel' that the community is determined to retain and emphasize. The first Activity Focus should therefore be aimed at cementing Bridge Road as the 'Main Street' of the Hobe Sound community. CRA actions should therefore be aimed at a consensus design approach to revitalize and support businesses.

There is also a great desire to actively and positively affect the Banner Lake Community. The second Activity Focus should be placed on a gradual beautification and infrastructure effort in Banner Lake.

Hobe Sound 2

Stormwater Design Toolkit

In 2012, the CRA amended the Master Stormwater and Utility plan to encourage sustainable development practices. The Stormwater Design Toolkit serves to demonstrate how the natural environment can be incorporated into redevelopment efforts in a positive way.

This plan was funded in part with a Grant From the South Florida Water Management District with the purpose of supporting the implementation of these tools for future public investments.

This plain language document identifies stormwater best management practices which enhance both the built and natural environment. The management practices outlined often result in significant cost savings upon implementation, as demonstrated by projects such as Mapp Road in the Palm City and Bridge Road in Hobe Sound.

The Stormwater Design Toolkit was showcased during a staff presentation at the American Planning Association - Florida Chapter annual conference sessions held September 2012.

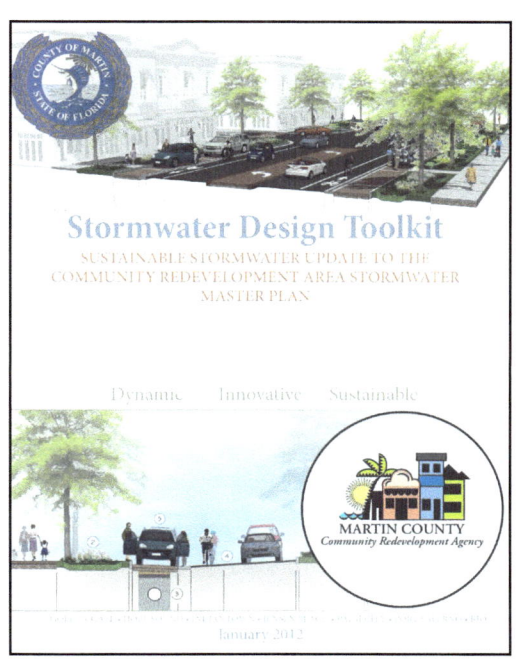

Bridge Road Town Center

Hobe Sound Sewer Project

In 2004, the Community Redevelopment Agency began to plan for the Hobe Sound Sewer project which would provide public utilities to the commercial properties on Dixie Highway and Bridge Road. The planning not only included the expansion of the utilities but also the physical design of both Dixie Highway and Bridge Road. In 2005, the CRA in coordination with South Martin County Utilities began the engineering design of the project.

In 2007, the planning and engineering was complete. The Hobe Sound downtown sewer project is the first major capital improvement accomplished in any of the CRA areas in the 9 years in Martin County and required a planning and funding strategy to maximize the Community Redevelopment Trust Fund in the CRA.

The ultimate cost to install the sewer and make all of the roadway improvements exceeded the available funding, so the project was intentionally phased. The first phase included the necessary underground waste water system. Staff would work on right of way acquisition, and additional funding sources for future surface level improvements.

The installation of the wastewater line was completed by 2008, which provided service to over 70 businesses and several single family lots that back onto Post Office Alley.

Design Vision

In 2009 the CRA began to explore the next steps to implement the community vision for Bridge Road. During this analysis several small demonstration projects were implemented. The first was the addition of 10 parallel on-street parking stalls on Bridge Road.

These spaces facilitated the facilitated leasing of vacant office/retail space which attracted more than $90,000 of private investment, the county reported lower speeds on Bridge Road, and the community became very engaged and focused on implementing more improvements on Bridge Road.

November 2010, the Hobe Sound NAC prioritized the improvements to the Bridge Road, and requested the formal design process to begin.

This work started with a public workshop in February 2011 with property owners and business owners along the Bridge Road Corridor. Staff listened to the community and staff developed two to three conceptual drawings for each property in conjunction with the individual property owner or business owner. These sketches were prioritized over the next several months and formed the basis of the conceptual plan for the corridor.

With the community consensus on the vision, the CRA contracted with Kimley-Horn in May for 2011 to prepare a more detailed concept plan. In September 2011, the conceptual plan was proposed and unanimously accepted by the Hobe Sound Neighborhood Advisory Committee.

The Plan included the following project Priorities:
1. Safety for vehicles and pedestrians
2. The same if not more parking
3. Undergrounding of aerial utilities
4. Provide for stormwater management facilities
5. Aesthetic improvements along the corridor

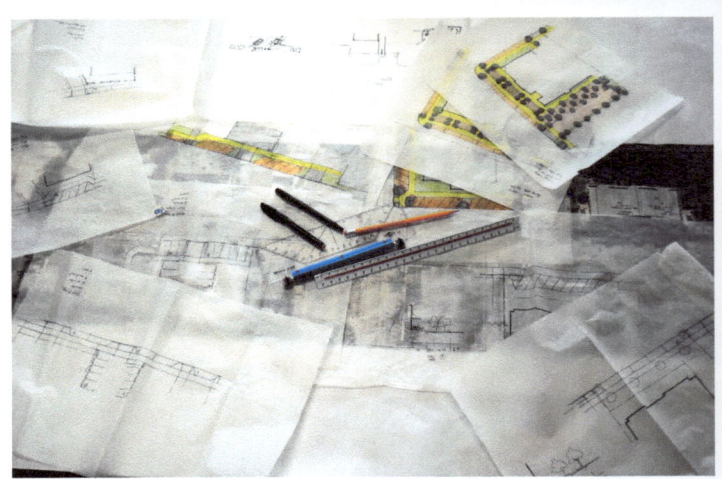

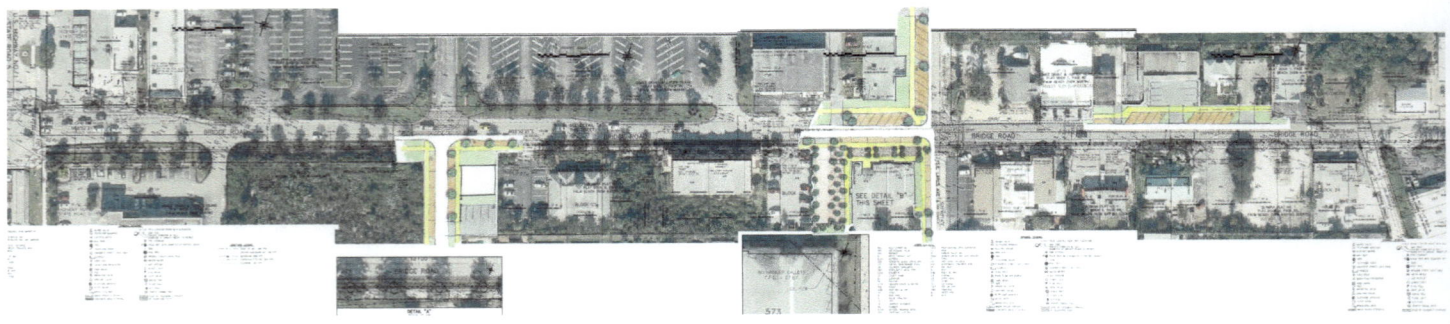

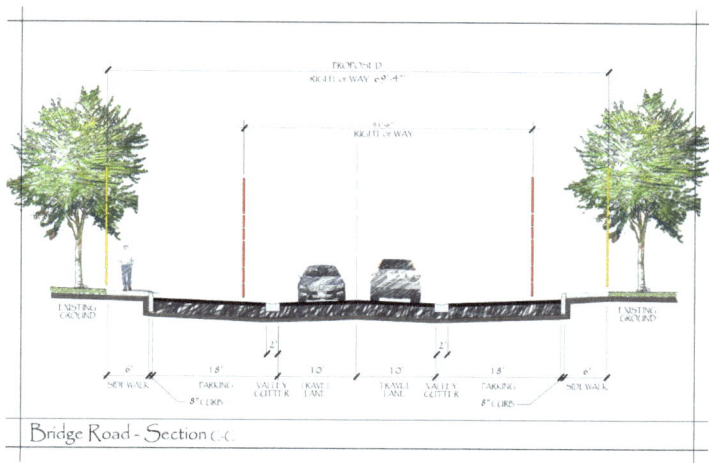

Bridge Road - Section C-C

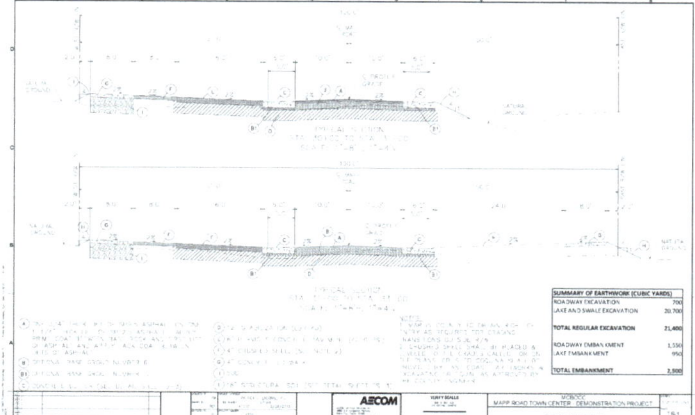

Engineering Design

In November 2011, the CRA contracted with Kimley Horn to prepare full design plans, which included Environmental analysis, geotechnical report, title search and right of way abandonment were completed in cooperation with Martin County Engineering Survey and Property Management Division. These plans would include a design that could be constructed in phases. The initial design would include the build-out of Bridge Road. The design could be implemented as property owners agreed to donate right of way, and as funding became available.

On May 8, 2012, The Martin County Board of County Commissioners approved the acceptance of all future Right-of-Way donations along Bridge Road. In October 2012, Kimley Horn had submitted 60% drawings for review by Martin County.

During the spring of 2014 staff met with property owners and business owners along the Bridge Road Corridor to and provided detailed design including parking, signage and streetscape enhancements for each property along with the corridor design plan. The staff continued to work with property owners in addressing their site specific concerns.

Property Management

The Hobe Sound Bridge Road "Main Street" project will provide enhanced street design requiring varying sizes of additional ROW (4' - 28') for the roadway, on-street parking, sidewalks and landscaping.

The project is based upon the voluntary donations for the addtional ROW's from the adjacent land owners.

On May 8, 2012 - The Martin County Board of County Commissioners approved the acceptance of all future ROW donations from the twelve property owners and authorized to execute any and all documents necessary to complete the transactions.

In late 2012, staff met with the property owners to help them understand how and why their property is being affected and acquired.

In 2014, staff began initial phase of negotiations by providing contract to purchase the necessary property and sketch showing the effect of the acquisition.

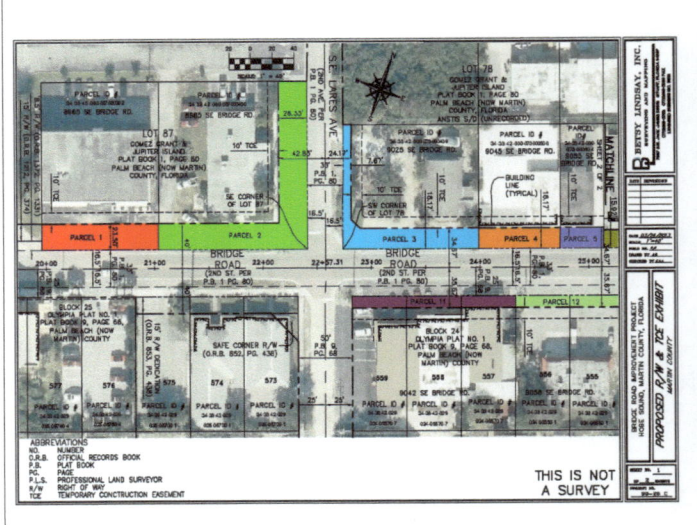

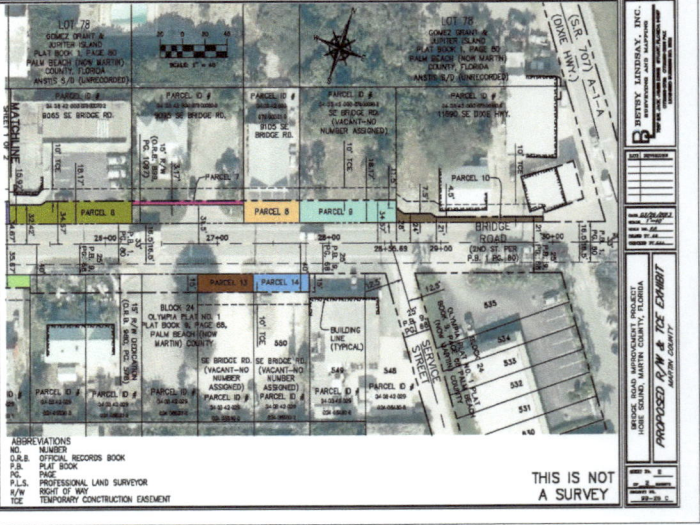

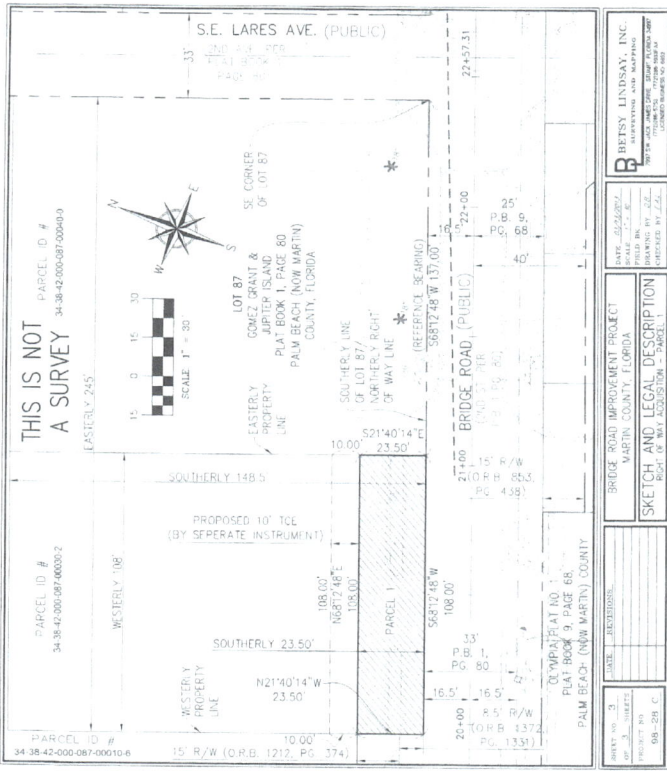

IMPROVED CONDITIONS - PARCEL 1

2

Utility Coordination

Throughout the design process staff had meet with all of the representatives of the franchise utilities along Bridge Road. These meetings provided staff the insight on the existing conditions, and provided the utility providers ample awareness of the proposed project.

In 2012, Staff met with South Martin Regional Utilities (SMRU) to discuss the proposed Bridge Road Improvement Project. They shared that there were several water services on Bridge Road, dating back to the 1920's. Through this coordination they shared their desire to replace the waterlines on Bridge Road. This provides a cost savings and an opportunity to replace the water service lines that are outdated.

Staff also met with FPL where several options were explored to harden and underground their service lines. FPL identified several locations where easements would need to be acquired on private property such as the parcel located in the Bridge Road/Lares Avenue. This easement would to provide for the necessary location for a transformer box, and would remove sight line impediments from the Bridge Road/Lares Avenue.

The planning staff in the Community Development Department was able to coordinate this request with the property owner by illustrating how this easement could improve the development potential for this site.

Innovative Design

The existing conditions along Bridge Road requires innovative engineering designs that meet new Florida Department of Transportation (FDOT) Traditional Neighborhood Design Standards (TND), which have not been adopted by Martin County. In June 2014, The NAC made a motion to request the County Engineer to support the application of FDOT TND standards to the Bridge Road Improvement Project.

Building on the work found in the Stormwater Toolkit, our consultant was able to design an innovative stormwater management system for Bridge Road. The South Florida Water Management District supported this innovation and actually referenced the Martin County Stormwater Toolkit detail sheets.

By July 2014 90% construction drawings were complete. Due to limited TIF funds, the project will be completed in phases. Staff worked with the NAC to prioritize the phasing of this project. Phase I will include the undergrounding of utilities which is a required first step, improvements at the intersection of Bridge Road and Dixie Highway which is a safety and transportation bottleneck. Additional phases are to be completed as additional TIF funds become available, and as properties redevelop.

Hobe Sound CRA - Bridge Road Redevelopment Plan

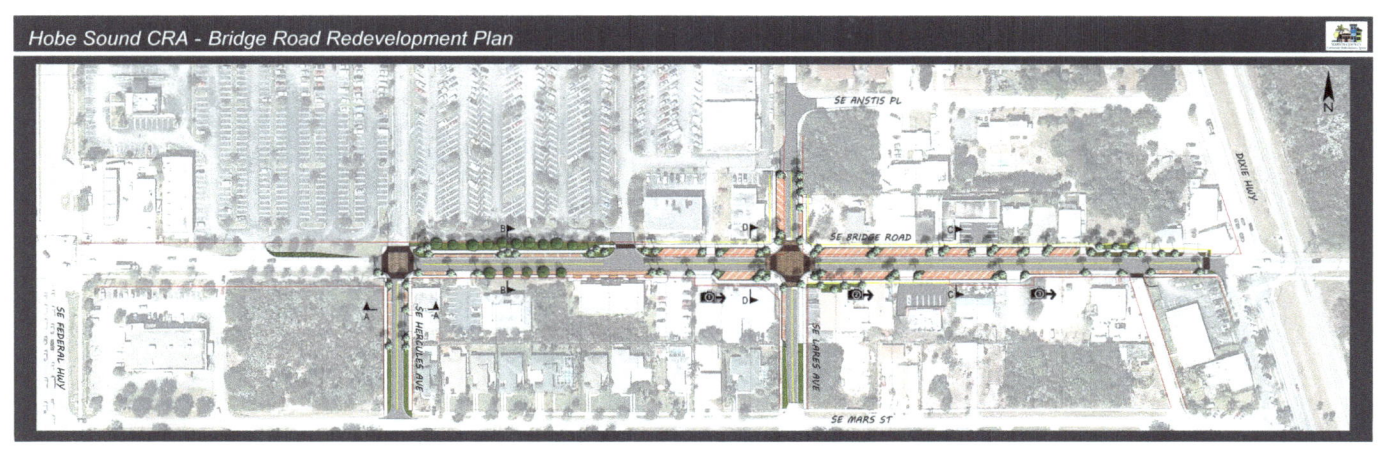

Hobe Sound CRA - Bridge Road Existing Conditions

Hobe Sound CRA - Bridge Road Redevelopment Plan

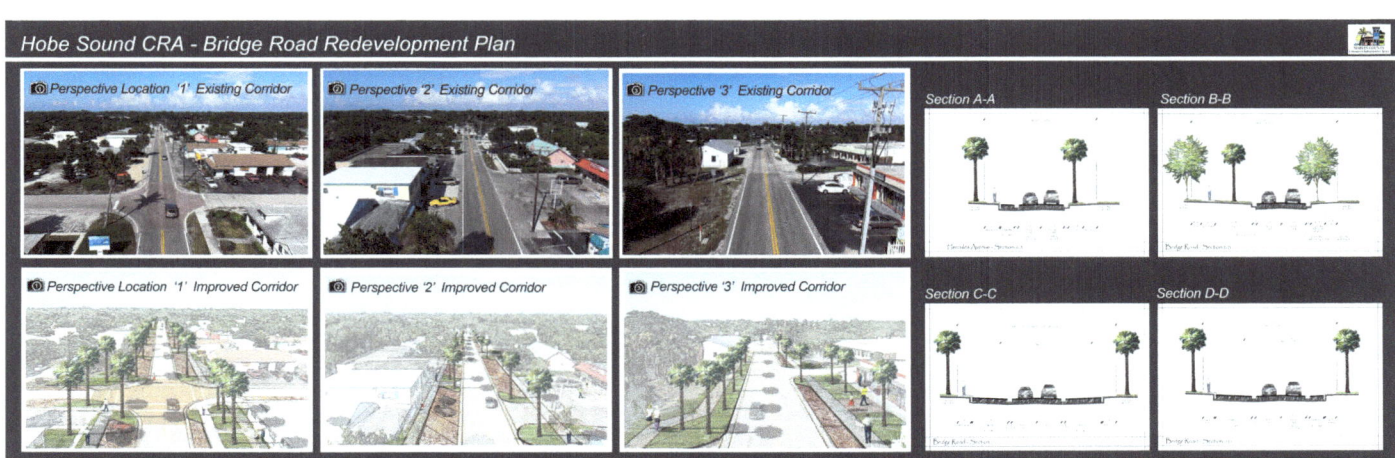

Implementation

Incremental Implementation

The Community Redevelopment Plan establishes a long term community vision for the future of the redevelopment area. The Community Development Department seeks opportunities to advance this vision with each capital investment through adaptive innovation. This lean approach to infrastructure supports the implementation of the community vision incrementally over time.

FEC Parking

In 2005, the Community Redevelopment Agency coordinated with local businesses and property owners to construct 25 additional on-street parking on Dixie Highway near Bridge Road. This project included a negotiated land lease with the Florida East Coast Railway, the repaving, restriping, and new landscaping, to the frontage road from Bridge Road to Apollo Avenue.

The construction of this project included funding from the Tax Increment Financing (TIF) and allocated District from Commissioner Weberman.

In 2006 the Florida Redevelopment Association (FRA) recognized Martin County's CRA for this project.

Post Office Alley

The CRA partnered with Martin County Engineering to pave Post Office Alley with pervious asphalt. This project used innovative stormwater management tools to reduce County maintenance, prevent washout, and provide a paved surface for deliveries to businesses on A1A/Dixie Highway. This project was identified through the Bridge Road workshops by business owners, property owners, residents, and staff.

Pervious Asphalt was identified as the best solution over standard asphalt paving. The total project cost is much lower, and the project time line was dramatically reduced. In addition, the material is easy to install and can be readily removed and reused as necessary.

The average cost of an asphalt roadway with typical stormwater management practices is $1 million a linear mile. This includes fees for engineering services, permitting, infrastructure such as pipes, gutters and curbing and cost of sub-grade materials. Innovative material choices like pervious asphalt can be installed directly over a dirt road without the need for exhaustive engineering drawings, state permits and other underground and off-site infrastructure for a cost of $320,000.00 a linear mile. Innovative material choices like pervious asphalt demonstrates significant cost savings to Martin County residents in comparison to conventional practices.

Following the completion of this project, new commercial businesses opened on Dixie Highway. Both the Dixie Highway and Bridge Road businesses utilize this newly paved road for access and for service deliveries. By moving service an deliveries to the rear of these properties, the primary streets are less congested with these large trucks.

Above: *The two sections above show Post Office Alley prior to the installation of environmentally friendly pervious asphalt, and after the work is completed. Pervious asphalt is an effective means of managing stormwater runoff.*

Bridge Road Parking

In 2010, a request from several property owners was made to assist in finding additional parking and traffic calming on Bridge Road. This led to the design and implementation of a demonstration project of 10 on-street parking stalls on Bridge Road.

In addition to the addition of on-street public parking, stormwater features were added to alleviate flooding and provide water quality, and the county sidewalk was upgraded.

This was the first step in implementing the Bridge Road Plan. The project facilitated leasing of adjacent vacant office space which created more than $90,000 of private investment in tenant improvements.

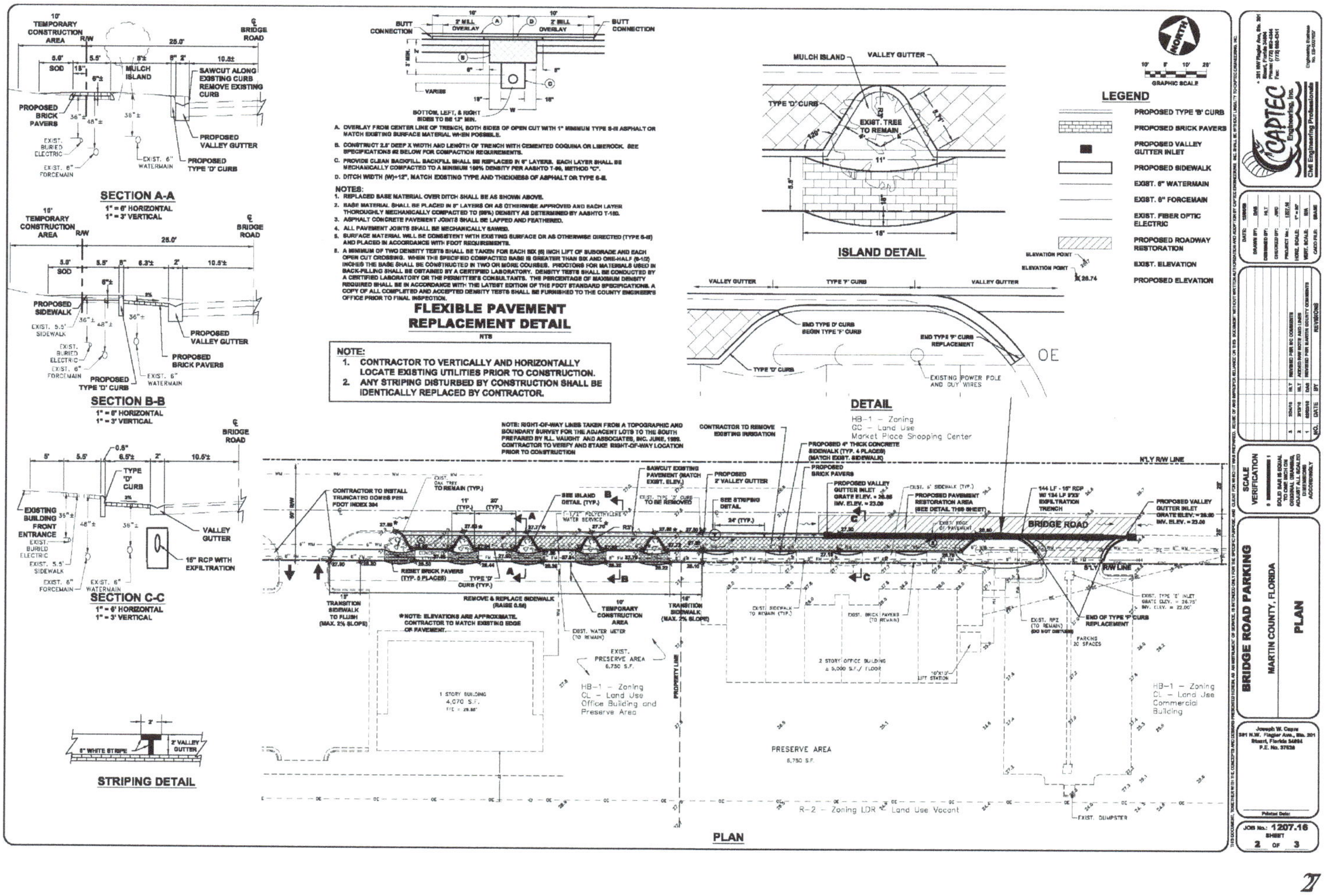

www.ingramcontent.com/pod-product-compliance
Lightning Source LLC
Chambersburg PA
CBHW060812290526

45792CB00005BA/1619